Tundra Experiments

14 Science Experiments in One Hour or Less

Last Minute Science Projects with Biomes

ROBERT GARDNER
ILLUSTRATED BY TOM LABAFF

Enslow Publishers, Inc.
40 Industrial Road
Box 398
Berkeley Heights, NJ 07922
USA

http://www.enslow.com

Library of Congress Cataloging-in-Publication Data:
    Gardner, Robert, 1929– author.
    Tundra experiments : 14 science experiments in one hour or less / Robert Gardner.
        pages cm. — (Last minute science experiments with biomes)
    Summary: "A variety of science projects related to the tundra biome that can be done in under an hour,
        plus a few that take longer for interested students"— Provided by publisher.
    Includes bibliographical references and index.
    ISBN 978-0-7660-5942-9
    1. Tundra ecology—Experiments—Juvenile literature. 2. Tundras—Experiments—Juvenile literature.
        3. Science projects—Juvenile literature. I. Title.
    QH541.5.T8G37 2015
    577.5'86078—dc23
                                        2013017301
Future editions:
Paperback ISBN: 978-0-7660-5943-6
EPUB ISBN: 978-0-7660-5944-3
Single-User PDF ISBN: 978-0-7660-5945-0
Multi-User PDF ISBN: 978-0-7660-5946-7

Printed in the United States of America
052014 Lake Book Manufacturing, Inc., Melrose Park, IL
10 9 8 7 6 5 4 3 2 1

To Our Readers: We have done our best to make sure all Internet Addresses in this book were active and appropriate when we went to press. However, the author and the publisher have no control over and assume no liability for the material available on those Internet sites or on other Web sites they may link to. Any comments or suggestions can be sent by e-mail to comments@enslow.com or to the address on the back cover.

♻ Enslow Publishers, Inc., is committed to printing our books on recycled paper. The paper in every book contains 10% to 30% post-consumer waste (PCW). The cover board on the outside of each book contains 100% PCW. Our goal is to do our part to help young people and the environment too!

Illustration Credits: Tom LaBaff (www.tomlabaff.com)

Photo Credits: ©1999Artville, LLC, p. 13; Shutterstock.com: Incredible Arctic, p. 29(left); NancyS, p. 29 (right); ©Thinkstock/iStock: afhunta, p. 6 (left); Robert Waltman, p. 6 (right); Gleichman, p. 8; Mihály Samu, p. 9; OlgaMiltsova, p. 19; Vladimir Melnik, p. 23; Ondrej Schaumann, p. 25; rusm, p. 27; Wheninusa, p. 31; John Pitcher, p. 36(both); ©Thinkstock/Purestock, p. 40

Cover Photo Credits: Shutterstock.com: ©Jason Stitt (young man); ©Marafona (mirror); ©ifong(ice cubes); ©Kichigin (snowflake); ©Pincarel (thermometer); ©Onur YILDIRIM (clock with yellow arrows); ©Thinkstock: JackF /iStock (polar bears); stativius/iStock (deer); Alexander Putyata/Hemera (globe)

Contents

LAST MINUTE Science Projects with Biomes

Indicates an experiment that features an idea for a science fair or project

Are You Running Late?

Do you have a science project that is due soon, maybe tomorrow? This book will help you! It has experiments about tundra biomes. Many of the experiments can be done in 30 minutes or less. An estimate of the time needed is given for each experiment. Maybe you have plenty of time to prepare for your next science project or science fair; you can still use and enjoy this book.

Many experiments are followed by a "Keep Exploring" section. There you will find ideas for more science projects. The details are left to you, the young scientist. With more time, you can design and carry out your own experiments, **under adult supervision**.

For some experiments, you may need a partner to help you. Work with someone who likes to do experiments as much as you do. Then you will both enjoy what you are doing. **In this book, if any safety issues or danger is involved in doing an experiment, you will be warned.** In some cases you will be asked to work with an adult. Please do so. Don't take any chances that could lead to an injury.

Tundra Biomes

A biome is a region of the earth with a particular climate. The plants and animals that live in a biome are quite similar all around the world. This book is about tundra biomes. But there are other biomes, too. Earth's land biomes include deserts, tundra, taiga, grasslands, rain forests, and temperate forests.

Tundra biomes cover one-fifth of the earth's land. That is an area equal to approximately 10 million square miles. Tundra stretches across the northernmost regions of North America, Europe, and Asia. The word *tundra* is related to a Finnish word meaning "treeless plain"—a brief, but reasonable, description of the biome.

Tundra biomes are found north of the taiga forests (see Figure 1 on page 13). They range from as far south as 55 degrees north latitude to well north of the Arctic Circle. Tundra biomes receive 4 to 20 inches of annual precipitation, not much more than some deserts. Nevertheless, tundra is damp with lots of marshy land in the summer. The reason for the moisture can be explained by doing Experiment 10 later in this book.

Winter temperatures range from a very chilly –57°C to –7°C (–70°F to –19°F). And the winds make it feel much colder. The ground is so cold that there is permafrost (permanently frozen ground) beneath the upper soil that melts in summer. The permafrost extends to a depth as great as 2,000 feet. During the brief summer, temperatures range between –1°C to 16°C (30°F to 60°F). With temperatures above freezing, there is about a foot of unfrozen tundra soil. But the permafrost prevents water from seeping very deep. The result is soggy ground. You can build a model of the permafrost in Experiment 5.

Buried in the permafrost are the preserved carcasses of thousands of woolly mammoths. A number of them have been removed and studied by biologists. Some scientists think it may one day be possible to produce a woolly mammoth using DNA from one of these frozen mammals.

The seasonal temperatures are related to sunlight. From mid-November until late January, much of the northern tundra never sees the sun. Then

The tundra in winter (left) and summer (right)

from late May until early August the sun never sets on this part of the tundra. However, light in the land of the midnight sun comes from a sun that moves close to the horizon. The sunlight travels a long path through Earth's atmosphere. And the atmosphere absorbs some of the light's energy. The light strikes the tundra at a low angle. This spreads its diminished energy over a wide area. (See Experiment 11.) Sunlight reaching the tundra is not very intense. However, it shines 24 hours a day for two months. Therefore, the tundra receives a significant amount of solar energy through June and July.

The soil is too shallow for trees to grow. Instead, the land is covered with a low growth of mosses, sedges, low shrubs, buttercups, poppies, saxifrage, and lichens. The roots of many of these plants survive the winter and foster new growth when spring arrives. There are also fast-growing plants that flower and make seeds quickly. Any plants that grow in the tundra are adapted for that biome. They have a short growing season, can endure low temperatures, and can grow in a shallow soil that lacks many nutrients and organic matter.

The variety of species that live in the tundra is more limited than in other biomes. Of the almost five thousand mammal species on the earth, only fifty live on the tundra. Many birds migrate to the tundra to feast on the insects that flourish there in the summer. The only year-round birds are ptarmigans, snow buntings, ravens, and snowy owls. Other animals that spend the winter include brown bears, polar bears, musk ox, arctic foxes, arctic ground squirrels, lemmings, voles, and weasels. In the seas near the tundra, we find whales, seals, walrus, and various fish.

The Scientific Method

To do experiments the way scientists do, you need to know about the scientific method. It is true that scientists in different areas of science use different ways of experimenting. Depending on the problem, one method is likely to be better than another. Designing a new medicine for heart disease and finding evidence of water on Mars require different kinds of experiments.

Despite these differences, all scientists use a similar approach as they experiment. It is called the scientific method. In most experimenting, some or all of the following steps are used: making an observation, coming up with a question, creating a hypothesis (a possible answer to the question) and a prediction (an if-then statement) designing and conducting an experiment, analyzing the results drawing conclusions about the prediction, and deciding if the hypothesis is true or false. Scientists share the results of their experiments by writing articles that are published in science journals.

You might wonder how you can use the scientific method. You begin when you see, read, or hear about something in the world that makes you curious. So you ask a question. To find an answer, you do a well-designed investigation; you use the scientific method.

Snowy owl

Once you have a question, you can make a hypothesis. Your hypothesis is a possible answer to the question (what you think is true). For example, you might hypothesize that because a tundra is damp, rainfall in a tundra is greater than in grassland. Once you have a hypothesis, it is time to design an experiment to test your hypothesis.

In most cases, you should do a controlled experiment. This means having two subjects that are treated the same except for the one thing being tested. That thing is called a variable. For example, to test the hypothesis above, you might measure the annual rainfall in a grassland and in a tundra for a decade.

you found that the rainfall in the grassland was significantly more than in the tundra, you would conclude that your hypothesis was wrong.

The results of one experiment often lead to another question. In the case above, that experiment might lead you to ask, what effect does less rainfall have on the kind of plants and animals we find in a tundra? Whatever the results, something can be learned from every experiment!

Science Fairs

Some of the experiments in this book have ideas that might be used as a science fair project. Those ideas are indicated with a symbol ( ) on the Contents page. However, judges at science fairs do not reward projects that are simply copied from a book. For example, a diagram of a leaf of grass would not impress most judges. However, an experiment that measured the effect of temperature on the growth rate of grass would attract their attention.

Science fair judges tend to reward creative thought and imagination. It is difficult to be imaginative unless you are really interested in your project. So, try to choose something that excites you.

Musk ox

And before you jump into a project, consider, too, your own talents and the cost of the materials you will need.

If you decide to use an experiment or idea found in this book as a science fair project, find ways to modify or extend it. This should not be difficult. As you do investigations, new ideas will come to mind. You will think of questions that experiments can answer. The experiments will make excellent science fair projects, especially because the ideas are yours and are interesting to you.

Safety First

Safety is very important in science. Certain rules should be followed when doing experiments. Some of the rules below may seem obvious to you, others may not, but it is important that you follow all of them.

1. Do any experiments or projects, whether from this book or of your own design, under the adult supervision of a science teacher or other knowledgeable adult.

2. Read all instructions carefully before proceeding with a project. If you have questions, check with your supervisor before going further.

3. Always wear safety goggles when doing experiments that could cause particles to enter your eyes. Tie back long hair and do not wear open toed shoes.

4. Do not eat or drink while experimenting. Never taste substances being used (unless instructed to do so).

5. Do not touch chemicals.

6. Do not let water drops fall on a hot lightbulb.

7. The liquid in some older thermometers is mercury (a dense liquid metal). It is dangerous to touch mercury or breathe its vapor. That is why mercury thermometers have been banned in many states. When doing experiments, use only non-mercury thermometers, such as digital thermometers or those filled with alcohol. If you have a mercury thermometer in the house, ask an adult to take it to a place where it can be exchanged or safely discarded.

8. Do only those experiments that are described in the book or those that have been approved by an adult.

9. Maintain a serious attitude while conducting experiments. Never engage in horseplay or play practical jokes.

10. Remove all items not needed for the experiment from your work space.

11. At the end of every activity, clean all materials used and put them away. Then wash your hands thoroughly with soap and water

A Note About Your Notebook

Your notebook, as any scientist will tell you, is a valuable possession. It should contain ideas you may have as you experiment, sketches you draw, calculations you make, and hypotheses you suggest. It should include a description of every experiment you do, the data you record, such as volumes, temperatures, masses, and so on. It should also contain the results of your experiments, graphs you draw, and any conclusions you make based on your results.

30 Minutes or Les

Here are experiments about tundra biomes that you can do
30 minutes or less. If you need to complete a science proj
by tomorrow, there's not much time left. So let's get starte

1. Using Maps (20 minutes)

What's the Plan?

Let's find out where tundra biomes are located around the world. And let's find out in which type of biome you live.

WHAT YOU NEED:

- map of biomes in Figure 1
- map of the world or large world globe

What You Do

1. Examine the map in Figure 1 on page 13. It shows where tundra and other biomes are located.

2. Look at the places where tundra biomes are found. Compare them with the same places on a map of the world or on a world globe.

3. On which continents does tundra exist? Are there continents that do not have a tundra biome?

4. Find where you live on a world map. Using Figure 1, find the biome in which you live.

What's Going On?

You compared the map of biomes in Figure 1 with a map of the world. You could see that tundra biomes are not found in Africa, Australia, South America, or Antarctica. They exist only in the northernmost parts of North America, Europe, and Asia.

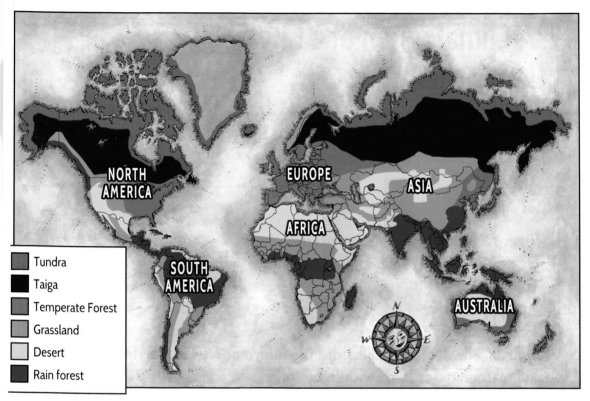

Tundra

Taiga

Temperate Forest

Grassland

Desert

Rain forest

Figure 1. The world's land biomes.

By a similar comparison, you could see in which type of biome you live. Don't be surprised if you think the map of biomes for your home is wrong. The map shows what is true for much of the region where you live, not every part of it. For example, the author lives on Cape Cod in Massachusetts. The biome map indicates that he lives in a temperate forest biome. However, the outer end of Cape Cod is covered by sand dunes. Also, while forest covers much of Cape Cod, the trees are shorter than in a typical temperate forest. This is caused by the strong winds and salt air coming off the Atlantic Ocean.

7. Greenland's Melting Ice Sheet (30 minutes)

What's the Plan?

During Greenland's summer, the sun's heat creates lakes on parts of its glaciers. One of these lakes may suddenly disappear. Scientists say that the lake water melts ice under the lake faster than the ice exposed to the air. The melted ice flows through a crack in the glacier to the bedrock under the glacier. The melted ice then acts like a lubricant, speeding the glacier's movement to the sea.

Can ice exposed to cold water melt faster than ice exposed to air? Let's do an experiment to find out.

What You Do

1. Obtain two ice cubes identical in size and shape.

2. Put one ice cube in a cup exposed to air.

3. Put the other ice cube in a large pan of cold tap water.

4. Watch the ice cubes. Which one melts faster?

What's Going On?

You probably found the ice cube in cold water melted much faster than the ice cube in warm air. Even though the water was colder than the air, a gram of water can provide about four times as much heat per gram as air when it cools one degree Celsius. Furthermore, the mass of air in contact with the ice cube was far less than the mass of water touching the ice. Consequently, the water, even though cold, provided much more heat to the ice than the air.

Keep Exploring–If You Have More Time!

- If you place ice cubes in water, does the time to melt the ice depend on the volume of water? Do an experiment to find out.

- If the volume of several pieces of ice is the same, does the shape of the ice affect the time for them to melt? How can you find out?

- If they have the same volume, which will melt faster, a cube of ice or a pancake-shaped piece of ice?

A glacier lake in Greenland

8. Seasons in the Tundra
(30 minutes)

WHAT YOU NEED:
- 2 T–pins
- white styrofoam ball
- sunlight or a single lightbulb in a dark room.

What's the Plan?

Let's use a model to show summer's 24 hours of light and winter's 24 hours of darkness in much of the tundra.

What You Do

1. Insert T-pins into opposite sides of a white styrofoam ball. The ball represents Earth; the T-pins represent Earth's north and south poles (Figure 6a).

2. Hold the ball in sunlight or several feet from a single lightbulb in an otherwise dark room. Hold the ball so that the light shines on it as shown in Figure 6a. This is the way Earth and Sun are oriented at the equinoxes around March 21 and September 21. As this model shows, the sun is very low in the sky over the tundra.

3. Tip the ball about 23 degrees (Figure 6b). This is the way Earth and Sun are oriented at the beginning of summer around June 21. Turn "Earth" slowly about its axis. Notice that much of the tundra will be in sunlight for 24 hours each day.

4. Tip the ball about 23 degrees the other way from its original position (Figure 6c). This is the way Earth and Sun are oriented at the beginning of winter around December 21. Turn "Earth" slowly about its axis. Notice that much of the tundra will be in darkness for 24 hours each day.

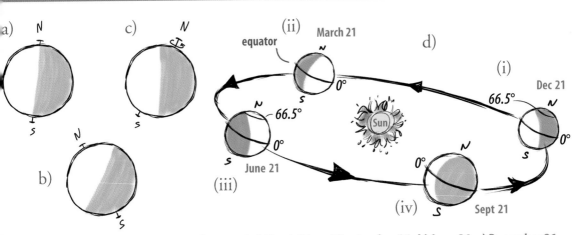

Figure 6. How sunlight strikes the earth around a) March 21 and September 21; b) June 21; c) December 21. d) Earth is shown at different times in its yearly orbit about the sun. Seasons shown are for the Northern Hemisphere: i) winter; ii) spring; iii) summer; iv) autumn.

What's Going On?

Because Earth's axis is tipped 23.5 degrees, regions near the poles receive 24 hours of sunlight during part of the year and no sunlight during other months of the year (Figure 6d). During summer in the Northern Hemisphere, much of the tundra will receive sunlight for 24 hours each day. However, the sun is low in the sky. Its light has a long path through the atmosphere. Some of the solar energy is absorbed by Earth's atmosphere and never reaches the ground.

In the winter, there are months when the tundra receives no sunlight. Temperatures may fall to as low as –57°C (–70°F).

Keep Exploring–If You Have More Time!

* Build a model to show Earth and Sun as Earth orbits the Sun during a one-year cycle.

Summer sun at midnight over the Arctic Circle

9. Camouflage: Present But Out-of-Sight (30 minutes)

WHAT YOU NEED:

- **50 white and 50 colored soda straws**
- **scissors**
- **snow—covered lawn**
- **a partner**
- **clock or watch**

What's the Plan?

Many animals in a tundra use camouflage to avoid predators. Their color often matches their surroundings, making it difficult to see them. For example, in summer the rock ptarmigan's feathers are flecked with brown and gray. In winter, these birds have white feathers that match the snow-covered land. Let's do an experiment to see how camouflage can keep a predator from finding its prey.

What You Do

1. Gather about 50 white and 50 colored soda straws. Cut them in half.

2. Spread the straws over a snow-covered lawn.

3. Consider the straws to be the "prey." Ask a partner, who did not see you spread the straws, to be the "predator." Tell the predator that the prey are soda straws, but do not mention color. As predator, he or she will seek the soda straw prey.

4. After five minutes, collect the straws the predator has found. Do the same after ten minutes, and again after fifteen minutes. Keep the five, ten, and fifteen minute piles separate.

5. Count the number of white and colored straws in each pile. What can you conclude?

Rock ptarmigan plumage is different in winter (left) and summer (right).

What's Going On?

You probably found that initially the predator found many more colored than white prey. The white prey were protected by camouflage like the bird in the photograph. They blended with their white surroundings. The colored prey were more easily seen. Their color contrasted with the white snow. The same would be true of ptarmigans if they retained their summer colors.

Keep Exploring–If You Have More Time!

- Look for animals that exhibit camouflage such as a praying mantis or grasshopper. Look, too, for a walking stick, which mimics a stick.

10. Why Is a Tundra Wet When It Receives Little Rain? (1 hour)

WHAT YOU NEED:

- paper towels
- a sink
- cold water faucet
- a balance that can weigh to ± 1 gram
- pen or pencil
- notebook
- line in cool place
- warm room
- clock or watch

What's the Plan?

A tundra biome may receive about the same amount of rain as a desert. But a desert is very dry, while tundra is usually damp or wet. One reason is the tundra's permafrost that prevents water from draining deep into its soil. But there's another reason as well. Let's find out what it is.

What You Do

1. Wet two folded paper towels in a sink. Hold them under a running cold water faucet.

2. Open the towels. Let any excess water drain away into the sink.

3. Fold both towels. Then weigh each towel on a balance that can weigh to ±1 gram. Record the weight of each towel in your notebook.

4. Fully open both towels. Hang one on a line in cool (not freezing) air, perhaps in a garage or basement.

5. Hang the other towel in a warm place, such as a kitchen.

6. After one hour, reweigh each towel and record its weight. From which towel did more water evaporate?

What's Going On?

You probably found that more water evaporated from the towel that was in warm air. The cold tundra air reduces the rate at which water evaporates. That's another reason why soil, plants, bogs, and all things in a tundra biome are usually wet or damp.

Keep Exploring–If You Have More Time!

- Tundra is characterized by open land with relatively few trees. However, the sun that warms the tundra is always low in the sky. Design and do an experiment to show that the sun's altitude affects the rate at which water evaporates.

Tundra permafrost prevents surface water from draining, forming pools.

11. The Effect of Angle on the Absorption of Radiant Energy (1 hour)

What's the Plan?

Any sunlight reaching the tundra comes from a sun that is low in the sky. Let's see how the angle at which sunlight reaches the ground affects the amount of solar energy it delivers. Do this experiment **with an adult**.

WHAT YOU NEED

- **an adult**
- **paper**
- **table**
- **flashlight**
- **scissors**
- **black construction pap**
- **3 identical thermomete**
- **ruler**
- **heat lamp**
- **stapler or paper clips**
- **small blocks**

What You Do

1. Place a sheet of paper on a table. Shine a flashlight directly onto the paper as shown in Figure 7a. Now, tip the flashlight so the light strikes the paper at a grazing angle much like sunlight in the tundra (Figure 7b). How has the amount of light per area changed?

2. For a more quantitative experiment, cut three rectangles from black construction paper. The rectangles will be made into "pockets" to cover the bulb ends of three identical thermometers. The size of the pockets will depend on the kind of thermometer you use. However, the pockets should completely cover the bulbs and lower ends of the thermometers. The pockets can be held together with staples or paper clips. Place an identical thermometer in each pocket (Figure 7c).

3. Place the three thermometers equal distances from a heat lamp (Figure 7d). One thermometer should lie flat so that it is at 90 degrees to the light. A second should be perpendicular to the light; the third should be at an angle

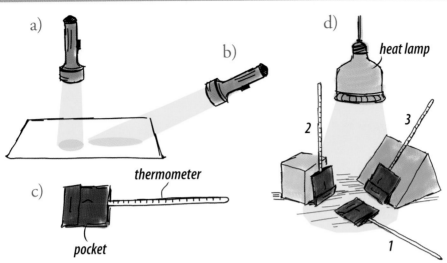

a)

b)

d)

heat lamp

2

3

thermometer

c)

pocket

1

Figure 7. a) Shine a flashlight on a sheet of paper from directly above and b) at a low angle similar to sun in the tundra. c) Make three pockets from black construction paper to cover the bulb ends of three identical thermometers. d) Place the thermometers about 30 cm (12 in) below a heat lamp as shown. Thermometer 1 is flat, at 90 degrees to the light. Thermometer 2 is parallel to the light at 0 degrees. Thermometer 3 is at about 45 degrees to the light. Use blocks to support thermometers 2 and 3.

of about 45 degrees to the light. Center the light over the thermometers at a height of about 30 cm (12 inches).

4. Just before turning on the heat lamp, all three thermometers should read approximately the same temperature. Watch the temperature on the flat thermometer. Turn off the lamp after 15 minutes or before the thermometer reaches its maximum temperature.

5. Read and record the three temperatures.

What's Going On?

You probably found that the flat thermometer at 90 degrees to the light had the greatest increase in temperature. The upright thermometer probably showed the least increase in temperature. These results confirm what you would expect when sunlight strikes the earth at different angles as you saw in step one of this experiment.

12. Surface Area, Volume, and Heat (1 hour)

What's the Plan?

Most animals living all year in tundra's cold climate are large. It's also true that their appendages (arms, legs, and ears) tend to be shorter than those of similar animals that live in other biomes. Let's see if we can figure out what advantage such features provide.

What You Do

Large animals with short appendages would have less surface area per volume than smaller animals with longer appendages. How does surface area per volume affect the flow of heat? Let's find out.

1. Find a plastic pill bottle or similar container that has a volume of about 100 mL. Also find a wide, shallow plastic container with a diameter of about 12 to 13 cm (5 in). Both containers should have covers.

2. Fill the pill bottle with water and pour it into the shallow container. Then fill the pill bottle again (Figure 8).

3. Cover both containers and carefully place them on a level surface in a freezer. Leave them overnight to let the water freeze.

4. Remove the two pieces of ice from the freezer. Drop both pieces of ice into a pail or dish pan containing a gallon or more of warm water. Which piece of ice melts faster?

Figure 8. These two containers hold the same volume of water; however, their surface areas are quite different.

What's the Further Plan?

You've seen how surface area per volume affects heat flow into something. Now let's see how it affects heat flow out of something.

What You Do

1. Fill a cup or drinking glass with hot tap water (about 40 to 50°C, or 100 to 120°F). Fill the plastic pill bottle or similar container with the hot water. Pour that water into the wide, shallow plastic container.

2. Again, fill the plastic pill bottle with the same amount of hot water. Place it beside the shallow wide container. If possible put both containers of hot water in a cool place such as a basement or outdoors if it's a cool (not cold) day.

3. Record the temperature of the water in each container at five-minute intervals for at least thirty minutes. In which container does the water lose heat faster? What can you conclude?

What's the Further Plan?

Let's see how an animal's size affects the ratio of surface area to volume. We'll let clay cubes represent animals.

Which animal has a larger surface area to volume ratio, a polar bear or an Arctic fox?

What You Do

1. Using clay, make a cube that is 1.0 cm on a side and a cube that is 2.0 cm on a side.

2. Calculate the volume and total surface area of each cube.

3. Calculate the ratio of surface area to volume for each cube. What happens to the ratio of surface area to volume as animal size increases?

What's Going On?

You probably found that the pancake-shaped ice melted faster than the cylindrical (pill-bottle) ice. Heat flowed faster into the ice with more surface area. The larger the surface area to volume, the faster the heat flowed.

You also probably found that the temperature of the water in the shallow, wide container cooled faster than the water in the cylindrical pill bottle. Heat flowed faster from the warm water that had more surface area exposed to the cooler air. Again, the larger the surface area to volume, the faster the heat flows.

Using clay cubes to represent animals, you saw that a bigger animal has a smaller surface area to volume ratio. The 1.0-cm cube had a volume of 1.0 cubic centimeter (cm^3). Its surface area was 6 square centimeters (cm^2) because each of its six sides had an area of 1.0 cm^2. Its surface area to volume had a numerical value of 6:1. The 2.0-cm cube had a volume of 8 cm^3 (2 cm x 2 cm x 2 cm) and a surface area of 24 cm^2. Its surface area to volume had a numerical value of 24:8 or 3:1. Because of surface area to volume, bigger animals lose heat more slowly than smaller animals. Consequently, they are better adapted to life in the cold tundra.

13. Insulated Winter Shelters (1 hour)

What's the Plan?

To escape the harsh tundra cold, some animals build shelters using wood chips, leaves, or other materials. Let's do an experiment to see if such materials provide insulation.

What You Do

1. Gather some wood chips and some old, dead leaves. Because tundra leaves are small, you should break or use scissors to cut the dead leaves into small pieces.

2. Fill a container with the wood chips; fill another identical container with leaves. Plastic containers such as 16-ounce cottage cheese containers should work well.

3. Find three smaller identical containers that will hold approximately 100 mL of water. Pill bottles from a pharmacy work well. Place one of these in each of the containers that hold wood chips or leaves. Hollow out a space so that the containers are surrounded by the leaves or wood chips (Figure 9a).

4. Fill a pitcher with very hot tap water. Nearly fill each of the three small (100 mL) containers with the hot water. The third container will

WHAT YOU NEED:

- wood chips
- dead leaves
- scissors
- 3 containers such as the 16–ounce plastic containers in which cottage cheese is sold
- 3 containers with about a 100 mL volume (plastic pill bottles work well)
- pitcher
- very hot tap water
- thermometer (1 or more)
- notebook
- pen or pencil
- watch

serve as a control. It will sit in air with no insulation (Figure 9b). These containers will each represent a small mammal living in the tundra biome.

5. Use a thermometer (one or more) to measure and record the initial water temperature in each small container.

6. Continue to measure and record these water temperatures every five minutes for at least 30 minutes. What can you conclude?

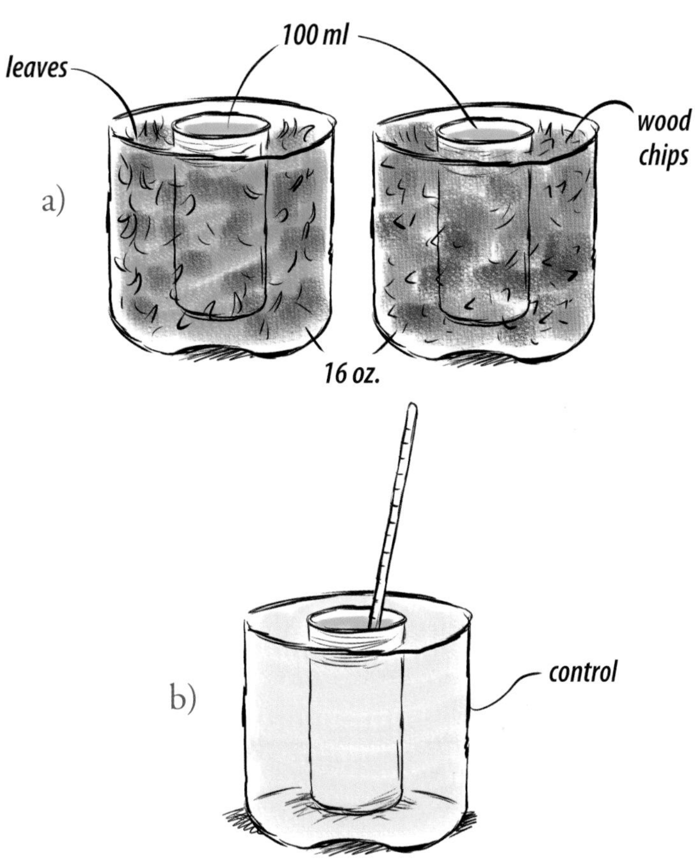

Figure 9. Will leaves or wood chips provide insulation for animal shelters?

What's Going On?

You probably found that the temperature of the water in the containers surrounded by wood chips or leaves decreased more slowly than the water exposed to air. You would conclude that these materials do provide insulation. Which material was the better insulator?

Keep Exploring–If You Have More Time!

• Does the thickness of the insulation make a difference? Do an experiment to find out.

14. A Way to Survive Tundra's Cold Temperatures (1 hour)

WHAT YOU NEED:

- **2 identical half–pint bottles**
- **very hot tap water**
- **heavy piece of fur**
- **large container**
- **cool place, if possible**
- **2 thermometers**
- **watch or clock**
- **notebook**
- **pen or pencil**

What's the Plan?

The skin of many animals that live in the tundra is covered with a heavy coat of fur. Let's do an experiment to see how fur helps keep an animal warm.

What You Do

1. Nearly fill two identical half-pint bottles with very hot tap water. Leave one bottle in the air. Surround the other bottle with a heavy piece of fur. You can secure the fur snugly around the bottle by placing both in a larger container (Figure 10).

2. If possible, place both in a cool place. Record their initial temperatures.

3. Record the temperature in each bottle of water every five minutes for at least half an hour.

4. Examine your data. What can you conclude?

A harp seal is coated with fur.

40

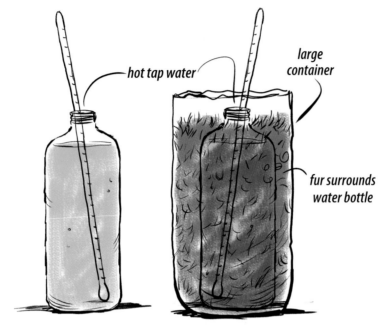

hot tap water

large container

fur surrounds water bottle

Figure 10. Is fur a good insulator?

What's Going On?

You probably found that the water surrounded by fur cooled more slowly than the water exposed to cool air. The fur acts as an insulator. It slows the flow of heat from a warm body, such as that of an animal, to the cooler surrounding air. Furry tundra mammals can stay warm. Their production of body heat can keep up with the heat they slowly lose to the cold air.

Keep Exploring–If You Have More Time!

- Some birds such as rock ptarmigans and snowy owls also survive tundra winters. Can feathers provide good insulation? Do an experiment to find out.

- Whales and seals live in the cold ocean water. They have a thick layer of blubber (fat) under their skin. Can fat provide good insulation? Do an experiment to find out.

1 hour or more

More Than One Hour

This remaining experiment takes longer. If you are a budding scientist, or have more than an hour to spend on your project, this experiment will be worth the time!

15. Snow as an Insulator (4 hours)

WHAT YOU NEED:

- 2 small plastic containers (with covers) having a volume of about 100 mL (large pill containers from drug stores work well)
- large nail
- warm water
- graduated cylinder or metric measuring cup

- 2 thermometers (–10–50°C or –20–120°F)
- 2 large plastic containers
- snow
- freezer
- clock or watch
- pen or pencil

- notebook
- graph paper
- 3 identical ice cubes
- 3 small, clear, plastic bags
- twisties
- 2 large plastic cups
- 2 (foam) coffee cups

What's the Plan?

Large animals are better adapted to survive in a cold climate than are small animals. However, small animals such as lemmings and voles live in the tundra. You probably won't see them during the long tundra winter. Where are they?

Many small animals burrow deep into the snow. The snow insulates them from the much colder air above. Can snow really serve as insulation? Let's do experiments to find out. First, we'll see if snow can slow the flow of outgoing heat. Then we'll experiment to see if it can reduce the flow of incoming heat.

What You Do

1. Find two 100 mL containers like those described in What You Need. Add about 70 mL of warm water to each container. Place covers on the containers. Use a large nail to make holes in the center of the covers so lab thermometers can be inserted into the containers. Insert a thermometer through each cover. The bulb should be near the middle of the water in each container (Figure 11a). Put one small container in a larger plastic container.

2. Add snow to the bottom of the other larger container. Place the other small container on the snow. Then surround the sides and top of the small container with more snow (Figure 11b).

3. Put both large containers and their contents into a freezer. Record the water temperature in each container initially and at ten-minute intervals. When water in both containers reaches 0°C (32°F) or the temperature stops decreasing, remove them from the freezer. Water freezes at 0°C (32°F).

4. Using your data, plot temperature versus time for both containers. Do both plots on the same graph. (See Figure 11c). What evidence do you have to indicate that snow is an insulator?

What's Going On?

Your graphs probably show that the temperature changed more slowly in the container surrounded by snow than in the one surrounded by air. This indicates that heat flows out of the snow-covered water more slowly than it does from water surrounded by cold air.

Now let's see if the same is true when heat flows into something.

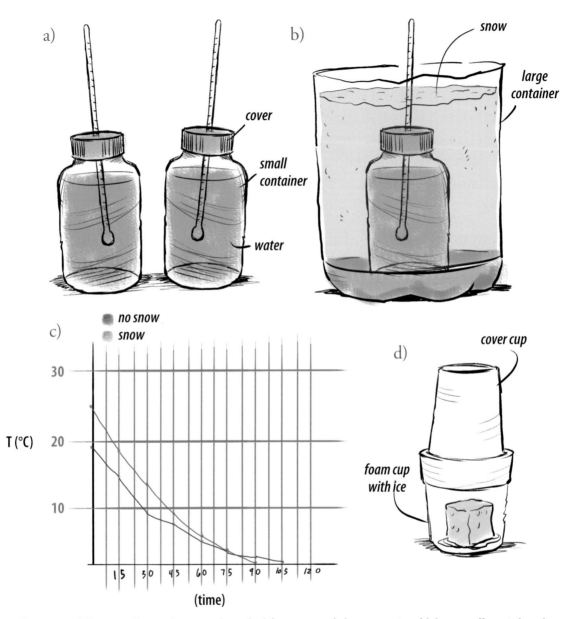

a)

cover

small container

water

b)

snow

large container

c)

■ no snow
■ snow

T (°C)

30

20

10

15 30 45 60 75 90 105 120

(time)

d)

cover cup

foam cup with ice

Figure 11. a) Two small containers equipped with water and thermometers b) One small container is placed in a larger container and surrounded with snow. c) Data and a graph of the data collected by the author when he measured water temperatures over a two-hour period for the two containers, one of which was covered with snow. d) Drawing that shows cup 2, which is a foam cup holding the ice. It is covered by a second foam cup.

What You Do

1. Put three identical ice cubes in small, clear, plastic bags. Squeeze the bags to remove air around the ice. Then seal the bags with twisties.

2. Place one ice cube in a plastic cup (cup 1). Place another in an insulated (foam) coffee cup (cup 2). Cover it with a second foam cup that has its upper third cut off (Figure 11d). Put snow in the bottom half of another plastic cup (cup 3). Put the third ice cube on the snow. Then add more snow to surround the ice and fill the rest of the cup.

3. Leave the three cups on a counter at room temperature. When snow in cup 3 begins to melt, remove it. Replace it with fresh snow.

4. Check the cubes and snow every few minutes. When the ice cube in cup 1 has completely melted, how big is the ice cube in cup 2? How big is the ice cube in cup 3?

What's Going On?

You likely found that snow kept the ice cube in cup 3 from melting as quickly as the ice in cup 1. Some ice may also have remained in cup 3 after the ice in cup 2 had melted.

Your experiments show that snow is an insulator. It slows the movement of heat out of warm matter (the water in the first experiment). And it slows the movement of heat into a cold substance (the ice in the second experiment).

Keep Exploring–If You Have More Time!

• On a cold winter day when there is plenty of snow on the ground, bury one thermometer on the ground under the snow. It should be attached to a string of bright yarn so you can find and retrieve it. Hang the other thermometer from a tree limb that is not in sunlight. After several hours, record the temperature on both thermometers. What can you conclude?

Words to Know

Arctic Circle—A latitude 23.5 degrees south of the North Pole or 66.5 degrees north of the equator.

biome—A region of the earth with a characteristic climate and species of plants and animals.

calorie—The quantity of heat needed to increase the temperature of one gram of water by one degree Celsius.

camouflage—An animal's coloring or structure that allows it to blend in with its surroundings. Camouflage makes it difficult for a predator to fin its prey.

climatogram—A graph that shows annual monthly rainfall and temperatu for a particular place on earth, such as a city or town.

concave mirror—A mirror with a saucer like surface that reflects light so a to bring it together.

Earth's axis—An imaginary line through Earth connecting the poles. Earth makes one turn about its axis every 24 hours.

evaporation—The change of a liquid into a gas.

glacier—A huge mass of ice that is drawn downward along a valley by gravity.

insulation—A material that reduces the rate at which heat flows from a warm substance to a cooler one.

permafrost—Ground that is permanently frozen.

solar energy—Light energy provided by the sun.

tundra—A cold, treeless biome where the subsoil is permanently frozen. The plants consist of low-growing shrubs, mosses, grasses, and lichens.

urther Reading

Benoit, Peter. *Tundra.* New York: Children's Press, 2011.

Davis, Barbara. *Biomes and Ecosystems.* Milwaukee: Gareth Stevens Publishers, 2007.

Levy, Janey. *Discovering the Arctic Tundra.* New York: Rosen Publishing Group's PowerKids Press, 2008.

Rhatigan, Joe, and Rain Newcomb. *Prize-Winning Science Fair Projects for Curious Kids.* New York: Lark Books, 2004.

Riggs, Kate. *Arctic Tundra.* Mankato, Minn.: Creative Education, 2010.

Tagliaferro, Linda. *Explore the Tundra.* Mankato, Minn.: Capstone Press, 2008.

Tocci, Salvatore. *Arctic Tundra: Life at the North Pole.* New York: Franklin Watts, 2005.

Wojahn, Rebecca Hogue. *A Tundra Food Chain: A Who-Eats-What Adventure in the Arctic.* Minneapolis, Minn.: Lerner Publications, 2009.

ternet Addresses

he Tundra Biome

<http://www.ucmp.berkeley.edu/glossary/gloss5/biome/tundra.html>

World Biomes: Tundra

<http://kids.nceas.ucsb.edu/biomes/tundra.html>

Index